facts

Water All Around

What Is Water?

by Rebecca Olien

Consultant:
Peter R. Jaffé, Professor
Department of Civil and Environmental Engineering
Princeton University
Princeton, New Jersey

Capstone
press
Mankato, Minnesota

First Facts is published by Capstone Press,
151 Good Counsel Drive, P.O. Box 669, Mankato, Minnesota 56002.
www.capstonepress.com

Library of Congress Cataloging-in-Publication Data
Olien, Rebecca.
    What Is water? / by Rebecca Olien.
    p. cm.—(First facts. Water all around)
    Includes bibliographical references and index.
    ISBN 0-7368-3704-3 (hardcover)
    1. Water—Juvenile literature. I. Title. II. Series.
GB662.3.O58 2005
551.48—dc22   2004010895

Summary: Introduces the basic elements of water and describes water as a liquid, a solid,
    and a gas.

Editorial Credits
Christine Peterson, editor; Linda Clavel, designer; Ted Williams, illustrator; Kelly Garvin,
    photo researcher; Scott Thoms, photo editor

Photo Credits
Brand X Pictures, cover
Bruce Coleman Inc./Janis E. Burger, 14
Corbis/Julie Habel, 12–13; Norbert Schaefer, 20
Folio Inc./Jeff Zaruba, 6
Gilbert S. Grant, 9
James P. Rowan, 16
RubberBall Productions/Alan Pappe, 5
Thinkstock, 18–19
Tom Stack & Associates Inc./Greg Vaughn, 10–11; Thomas Kitchin, 17
Wanda Winch, 15

1 2 3 4 5 6 10 09 08 07 06 05

Table of Contents

Water Is Everywhere

Earth is called the "water planet." More water than land covers the earth's surface. Salt water fills the oceans. Freshwater flows in rivers and lakes. Water freezes into ice and snow. It is found in air as clouds and fog. Water is all around us.

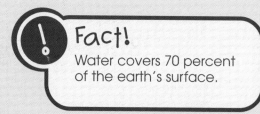

Fact!
Water covers 70 percent of the earth's surface.

Parts of Water

Water is made up of tiny parts called **atoms**. People cannot see atoms. Atoms join together to form **molecules**.

Water Molecule

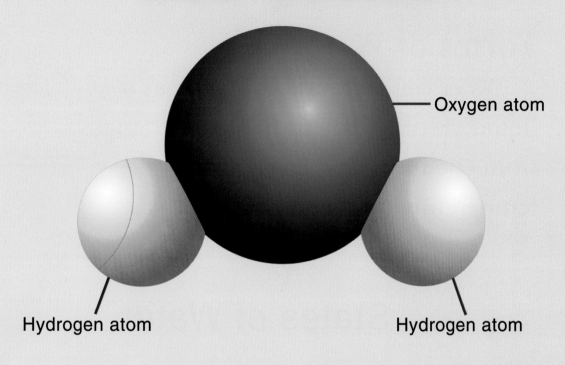

Oxygen atom

Hydrogen atom   Hydrogen atom

Millions of molecules are in one drop of water. A water molecule has two **hydrogen** (H) atoms and one **oxygen** (O) atom. Water is often called H_2O.

Forms of Water

Water can be found in nature as a liquid, a solid, and a gas. Water changes from one form to another as the temperature rises and falls.

States of Water

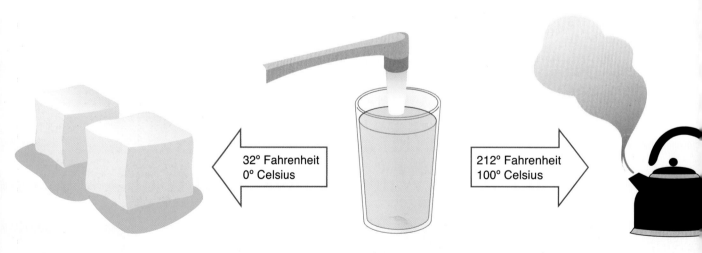

| Solid | | Liquid | | Gas |

32° Fahrenheit
0° Celsius

212° Fahrenheit
100° Celsius

Water's three forms can be found in nature. Water splashes in waves as a liquid. A chunk of ice is solid water. Clouds are water as a gas called **vapor**.

Water as a Liquid

Water is a liquid at most temperatures on the earth. Liquid water flows in rivers. It fills lakes and oceans. Liquid water trickles under the ground.

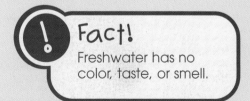

Fact! Freshwater has no color, taste, or smell.

Water as a Solid

Water becomes a solid when it freezes. Water changes into snow or ice below 32 degrees Fahrenheit (0 degrees Celsius). Snow forms when water vapor turns into solid crystals. Ice forms when liquid water freezes.

! Fact!
Every snowflake has six sides.

Water as a Gas

Heat changes liquid water into vapor. Water heated by the sun **evaporates**. It turns into a gas and rises into the air.

People can't see vapor. It is part of the air. Vapor is in the air people and animals breathe out. Plants give off water vapor through their leaves.

Salt Water and Freshwater

Most water on the earth is salt water. Salt water contains salt and other **minerals**. Oceans hold almost all of the world's salt water.

Freshwater makes up 3 percent of the earth's water. Land animals drink freshwater from lakes and rivers. **Glaciers** are made of frozen freshwater.

Water Covers the Earth

Water covers the earth. Oceans stretch across most of the planet. Glaciers packed with ice blanket the Arctic. Rivers, lakes, and streams flow across the land. Plant roots soak up water from under the ground. Water is all around.

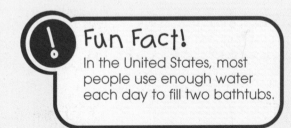

! Fun Fact!
In the United States, most people use enough water each day to fill two bathtubs.

Amazing but True!

Our bodies are about 70 percent water. Water is part of blood. Blood carries food and oxygen to parts of the body. Our brains and muscles are mostly water. Even bones are 22 percent water. Water is important for life and good health.

Hands On: Disappearing Drops

Water can be found in nature as a liquid, a solid, and a gas. Try this experiment to see how water changes from one form to another.

What You Need

waxed paper
water

What You Do

1. Sprinkle a few drops of water on a piece of waxed paper. You can scatter drops by shaking your wet fingers over the waxed paper.
2. Place the waxed paper in the freezer.
3. After about 15 minutes, take the drops out of the freezer. The water drops should be frozen.
4. Place the waxed paper in sunlight or under a bright light.
5. Watch the frozen drops change from solid to liquid.
6. Keep watching as the liquid drops seem to disappear. Where do the water drops go? The water is changing into invisible water vapor.

Glossary

atom (AT-uhm)—an element in its smallest form

evaporate (i-VAP-uh-rate)—the action of a liquid changing into a vapor or gas; heat causes water to evaporate.

glacier (GLAY-shur)—a large moving sheet of packed snow and ice

hydrogen (HYE-druh-juhn)—a colorless gas that is lighter than air and burns easily

mineral (MIN-ur-uhl)—material from the earth that is not a plant or an animal

molecule (MOL-uh-kyool)—the atoms making up the smallest unit of a substance; H_2O is a molecule of water.

oxygen (OK-suh-juhn)—a colorless gas in the air that people need to breathe

vapor (VAY-pur)—water in gas form

Read More

Gallant, Roy A. *Water.* Kaleidoscope. New York: Benchmark Books, 2001.

Neye, Emily. *Water.* All Aboard Science Reader. New York: Grosset & Dunlap, 2002.

Rosinsky, Natalie M. *Water: Up, Down, and All Around.* Amazing Science. Minneapolis: Picture Window Books, 2003.

Internet Sites

FactHound offers a safe, fun way to find Internet sites related to this book. All of the sites on FactHound have been researched by our staff.

Here's how:
1. Visit *www.facthound.com*
2. Type in this special code **0736837043** for age-appropriate sites. Or enter a search word related to this book for a more general search.
3. Click on the **Fetch It** button.

FactHound will fetch the best sites for you!

Index